ADVANCED RHINOCEROLOGY
"to help you through the jungle"

ADVANCED RHINOCEROLOGY

by Scott Alexander

Illustrations by Laurie Smallwood

Published by:
    The Rhino's Press
    P.O. Box 2413
    Laguna Hills, Ca. 92653
    (714) 997-3217

First Printing—October, 1981
Twelfth Printing—July, 1985

Library of Congress Catalog Card Number:
  81-51912
ISBN: 0-937382-01-9

CONTENTS

Chapter		Page
	Dedication	7
	Warning	9
	Introduction	11
1.	Don't Be A Cow	13
2.	It Is A Jungle Out There	21
3.	Meet Your Safari Guide	33
4.	The Hunt	39
5.	Quit Your Job	45
6.	The Fear of Being Squished	61
7.	The Free Enterprise Game	71
8.	An Entrepreneurial Safari	85
9.	The Rhinocerotic Revolution	91
10.	Jungle Education	109
11.	Epilogue	121

DEDICATED TO

Bob and Cynthia Alexander
L.J. Howard
Dr. Robert and Mary Lou Landes
Shylie Lewis
Paul, Karen and Heather Teague

WARNING!!!

The information contained in this book is recommended reading for rhinoceroses ONLY! If you are presently a cow, *DO NOT* read any further. YOU ARE OFF LIMITS! Please report back to your pasture and have a nice decay.

Thank you for your cooperation.

INTRODUCTION

Your breath takes on a hot, strong, muggy odor as your nostrils flare, expelling the air from your massive lungs. Within hours, sometimes minutes, you have gained six thousand pounds . . . hopefully distributed in the right places. Your skin tightens and becomes two inches thick. A horn starts to grow right out of your forehead while the muscles in your legs begin to twitch from all the excess energy coursing through your body. Suddenly, you feel the urge to let loose with your first rhino grunt. A loud, whining roar comes bellowing from deep within you and you take off charging. Another rhinoceros finds its way to the jungle!

Since the introduction of "Rhinoceros Success" in 1980, thousands have turned into rhinoceroses or, for the first time, realized that they were already rhinos. The decade of the rhinoceros is here. Achievement, prosperity, and most of all, happiness are the characteristics of the rhino. It IS a jungle out there, but you are ready for some adventure anyway, aren't you? Sharpen your horns and let's go do some charging!

Chapter 1

DON'T BE A COW

If you are looking for an easy way to success, an easy way to happiness, an easy road to riches, an easy out to anywhere, then this book is not for you. Quit looking. There is no easy road to success. A life of adventure, achievement and happiness is not for the thin-skinned and lazy.

Success is success because to achieve it is difficult. To say that success is easy is only cheating those who have become success-ful. If becoming successful was easy, if any-one could do it, it would not be success, would it? It would be mediocrity!

To be mediocre is easy. That's why there are so many people living mediocre lives. These people are the cows. They live their lives in the pasture following each other around day after day, year after year, complaining and rationalizing their dismal existence. Cows tend to procrastinate and never really accomplish anything their whole lives.

COWS ARE MISERABLE

That is not the most desirable way to spend the little bit of time you have here on earth. Life is an adventure, and an adventure is supposed to be fun, right? Cows just do not have fun. Have you ever seen a cow smile? Cows do not smile. They have trouble laughing too! I am sure that you have seen some of them. The government hires a lot of them to work in the Department of Motor Vehicles. What a wretched way to live! Of course, you can't blame them. I wouldn't smile either if I was a cow. The most exciting day for the cows is when they are all led off to the slaughterhouse.

RHINOS ARE HAPPY

Then there are the people who are doing everything. They are the rhinoceroses! The rhinos are the ones who are building up their own businesses, buying and selling all the real estate, travelling all over the world, raising happy rhino families, spending their lives doing what they enjoy doing, and living adventurous lives charging around in the jungle.

And it *IS* a jungle out there! Just watch the six o'clock news and you will see just what a jungle it is! Fortunately, it is not as bad as the TV and newspapers would have you believe. But there are certainly definite dangers and that is what makes it an adventure!

Adventures are fun because there is always that element of risk, the intrigue and suspense of the unknown. Sometimes you will get stuck in the mud. You simply accept it as part of the excitement and figure out how you are going to get out, rather than give up and sink like a cow would do. You are a rhinoceros! You love adventure! They will never find you wandering aimlessly in any pasture looking for a place to lie down.

Rhinoceroses are chargers! That's what rhinos are famous for: charging, taking action, moving, being full of energy. Once you have a damn-the-torpedoes rhinoceros spirit, once you start taking immediate action every day, you are on your way to wherever you want to go.

ACTION IS ESSENTIAL

There are many books that advocate having written goals and then visualizing your way to success. I do not believe that you can sit at home and visualize your way to success. That is a cow's fairy tale! A new Rolls-Royce will not come knocking at your front door because

"It is fun being a rhinoceros!"

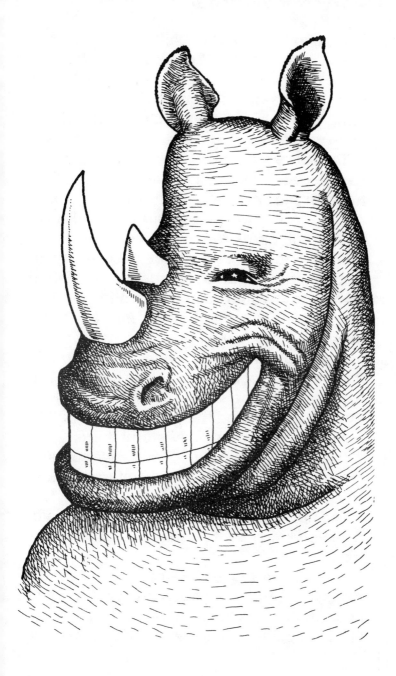

you sat at home and visualized it three times a day. That is against the laws of nature.

I *do* believe that visualizing the Rolls-Royce and then taking action to get it will one day bring the delivery man to the front door to hand you the keys. But again, the major key is CHARGING and I don't mean with the credit cards! Watch out for the killer bees . . . Buffums, Broadway, and Bullocks. If you get into trouble, go in for plastic surgery and have your credit cards removed!

I like to tell the story of the baseball scout who found a remarkable prospect. He found a horse that would get up to bat and ALWAYS hit the ball. This horse never missed! Naturally, the scout signed him on with one of the major league baseball teams. Sure enough, the first game of the season, the horse got up to bat and on the very first pitch – WHAM! – the horse smacked the ball way out into left field. Then the horse just stood there.

The manager jumped up and down screaming at the horse, "Run, you stupid horse! Run!"

The horse turned to the manager and said, "Are you kidding? If I could run, I'd be at the racetrack!"

You see, hitting the ball (having goals and a positive attitude) is important, but the most important part is to run! You don't want to be like the positive thinker who fell off the top of a ten story building and on his way down could be heard repeating, "Well, I'm O.K. so far!"

Think positively, study your bio-rhythms, keep knives out of your toaster, cross your fingers, keep your car's tires at the proper pressure, do everything and anything that could possibly help you, but above all, make SURE that you KEEP CHARGING!

EXPECT SOME TORPEDOES

Additional benefits that rhinoceroses enjoy include two inch thick skin and rhinoceros audacity. With a damn-the-torpedoes charging spirit, rhinoceroses are known to catch most of the torpedoes. The torpedoes are the problems, the set-backs, and the rejection that we are faced with every day. Hey! That comes with the territory! The jungle has no fences. There is no security. Even the cows are not totally secure lying in their pasture. Occasionally, torpedoes will dart in through the fences and finish a couple of them off. They don't have two inch thick skin like we do.

The best way to thicken your hide is to expose it to the torpedoes. After you have been hit a few times, your skin starts to toughen up. This doesn't mean that you are insensitive to others. In fact, rhinoceroses are known to be the most loving, helpful, and generous animals there are.

Rhinoceroses donate the money to build hospitals and universities. They build libraries and parks, and everything else that contributes to the betterment of the world. If anyone is insensitive to others it is the cows. They are non-producers who contribute nothing. The cows want to be taken care of and would like nothing better than to have the whole world sharing their stinky, manure-filled pasture. That is being insensitive!

AUDACITY IS FUN

Finally, you are audacious. Consider the football players. Do you think that they would be out there knocking each other around like that if they didn't have all their body pads and helmets on? No way! They would be a lot more cautious. It is their protective gear which allows them to play hard.

It is the same way being a rhinoceros. Your two inch thick skin is your protective gear. It lets you throw caution to the wind! You will do audacious things like invest all of your money in a new business, or quit a job that you have had for twenty years to sell real estate, or anything else that you have always wanted to do but have not had the guts or nerve to do. Remember, life is an adventure! It is fun to be audacious!

Chapter 2

IT IS A JUNGLE OUT THERE

Can you feel the urgency of it? Can you sense the excitement that the rawness, the uniqueness, and the vibrancy of the jungle generates? Do you see the opportunities here? Can you hear the unfamiliar sounds, the screams, the cries, the roaring and the laughter? Yes, life is a jungle.

Does the steamy heat make your blood pump faster? Does the confused bustle of activity arouse you? Do the long, cool, dark nights make you anxious? As the morning sunlight filters down through the overgrown thickets and lush vegetation to light a new day, do you feel the urgency to become a part of it all? The jungle is waiting.

"Rhinos love the jungle."

Your pulse quickens and seems to complete the jungle aura, beating with an intense, rhythmic forcefulness that brands you a member of this disordered and complex world. Sucking in a breath of damp, earthy air, your mind reels as you observe the size of it all. Can you feel the intensity, the constant stimulation, and the satisfaction of knowing where you are? You and the jungle have become one!

Nothing like a little drama to get the point across, right? Do you feel it now? Seriously though, it is a jungle out there, but that works out great because rhinos love the jungle! We are set up to work best in the jungle with our two inch thick skin, audacity, persistence, and energy.

NO ONE SAID IT WAS GOING TO BE EASY

Sure, there are unpleasantries and suffering. *No one said that the jungle was fair!* Of course, there is danger to life and limb. Getting killed, however inconvenient or displeasing that may sound to you, happens in the jungle ALL THE TIME. *No one said it was going to be safe!* Jungle life can at times be so frustrating that some, rather than wait to be killed, will kill themselves. *No one said it was going to be easy!*

So we've got sorrow and cruelty, pain and disease, and death and destruction as everyday occurrences in the jungle. Oh well. *No one said it was going to be boring!* Be thankful for that! It is all right to be sad, it's O.K. to be angry, go ahead and tremble with fear, it is permissable to cry out in anguish, and there is nothing wrong with being dead. But to live a life of boredom is worse than no life at all. Thanks to the jungle, you are never going to have to live a fate worse than death. Thanks to the jungle all you have to do is open your eyes, all you have to do is listen to what is happening around you, and I guarantee that you will NEVER be bored!

YOU NEVER KNOW FOR SURE

This jungle we live in is far from boring. There is little predictability. In fact, if there is anything that you can be sure of, it is unpredictability! Start your own business and what will happen? Who knows? You could become wealthy or you could become pitifully broke. Take a walk and what might happen? There is no telling! You might meet the most beautiful animal in the forest and have a steamy jungle affair, or you might get hit by a truck. Either way, you're in trouble there!

Just the simple task of getting your eight hours' sleep has a certain uncertainty about it. Maybe the old rhino heart will decide to quit while you are away in dreamland. Hearts don't work forever, you know. Occasionally, they go on strike.

What will you be doing in ten years? You can guess, you can postulate, you can theorize, but you can never be sure. In ten years, you might be one of the jungle's more unfortunate statistics or you could be living in ecstasy. You might own vast portions of the jungle and live in a magnificent home with your happy rhino family. Regular vacations to other jungles, where you are greatly respected, might be how you spend some of your time. You could be living the good rhino life complete with daily horn manicures, two-inch-thick skin massages, your own mudhole in the back yard, a first edition copy of "Advanced Rhinocerology," and a Rolls-Royce with your name on the license plate.

THE JUNGLE IS UNFAIR

It is a jungle out there and it is exciting! Sometimes it seems that there is evil and darkness out of necessity, for with every good there is a bad, for every acid there is an alkaline, and for every tear there is laughter. Yes, goodness does indeed abound in the jungle.

No one said that the jungle was fair and that is all right because when the jungle makes it rough for some, it allows others to give, which in turn, enriches everyone. One's misfortune allows another to appreciate and love where before there may have been a disinterest.

The jungle's unfairness provokes a compassion and a caring so deep that it would respond to no other stimulus. It provokes a pity that, without the jungle's blatant savagery, might never have been awoken from somewhere within our animalistic souls. Only the cruelty and violence of the jungle could bring forth the emotions of love and peace, of sharing and caring, and a determination to overcome the jungle's injustices that bring us all together as one.

JUNGLE LIFE CAN BE DANGEROUS

No one said it was going to be safe which, again, is fortunate. The hazards of the jungle make us wary and careful not to act foolhardy. It's fine to charge with a damn-the-torpedoes spirit because too much caution can be detrimental, but whatever you do, DON'T jump in front of the torpedoes when you can see them coming! Some of the bigger torpedoes can be avoided.

As a matter of fact, somewhere in the jungle is the biggest torpedo you have ever seen with your name on it and that is the one you want to avoid for as long as you possibly can! Don't spend time troubling yourself and fretting about it though, or you are liable to

"You could be living the good rhino life complete with two-inch-thick skin massages."

end up worrying yourself to death before it has a chance to get to you.

True, death and disease run rampant in the jungle, but then, so does abundant living and happiness. Besides, both death and life serve to remind us that this jungle is only a temporary safari while we wait to be with our Lord. If death does anything, other than eventually kill you, it should fill you with a love for God and a trust in Him so strong that death is the least of your worries.

LIVING IN THE JUNGLE IS CHALLENGING

Finally, no one said it was going to be easy, for with easiness comes laziness and with laziness comes boredom: *the ultimate death.* Thanks to the jungle, it is not easy. All evil is easy. Dying, cheating, losing, and mediocrity are all EASY! Stay away from easy!

All good is hard. All accomplishment is challenging. You are tough, so go with the tough stuff. Welcome difficult situations to strengthen you. Use uncertainty to solidify your faith. Utilize all of the jungle's difficulties as targets to charge down and stab with your horn. Problems are the jungle's method of giving you real satisfaction as you overcome and destroy them. This is your chance to use a little aggression. Don't just solve your problems, DEMOLISH them!

Can you imagine a jungle where everything was easy? We wouldn't be rhinos, we would be hippos! It *is* a jungle out there and it is challenging. Each day pulsates with energy and excitement and that is what rhinos thrive on. The cows can sit in their pastures where they try to live a risk-free existence, but eventually they will discover the folly of trading their freedom for their lives.

The jungle is wild, yes. The jungle can be ugly and perilous, true, but at the same time it can be awe-inspiring and richly rewarding. Best of all, the jungle is free.

Chapter 3

MEET YOUR SAFARI GUIDE

No safari through the jungle would be complete without a knowledgeable, experienced guide and I have got just the one you are looking for. Most of you probably already have Jesus Christ leading you on your expedition so you are all set, but for those of you who haven't had the time to look up a good safari guide or just plain forgot that you need one, here is the good news: through Jesus Christ, God can still fit you in to His schedule!

God is the ultimate protection against the dangers of the jungle and He has a keen sense of awareness. All the successful rhinos have God as their safari guide. Do not settle for any less! There are certain things that you just cannot afford to cut corners on and this is one of them. You can forget your canteen, but do not forget to make arrangements with God to guide you. Overlook your trail map, but make sure that God is always with you.

NOBODY DOES IT BETTER

Never accept any lesser, fly-by-night guides or your whole safari will end in tragedy. There are too many unexpected dangers that can confront you. Trekking through the jungle without God means confusion, hardships, frustration, and eventual death. Why subject yourself to all that when God is so available, so willing, and so easy to arrange for guidance on your safari? Besides that, He's a nice guy!

Remember that God created the jungle. No one knows it better than He does. It is His full time job to lead animals through the jungle and He would be hurt if you didn't ask Him for His help. He is very easy to get along with, He doesn't eat much food, He has a lot of contacts, He's available 24 hours a day, and He is capable of miracles!

SEND NO MONEY

To arrange for God to lead you on your safari, you don't have to telephone Him (God is the original wireless operator), you don't have to send Him a letter (sometimes you just can't wait that long), and you don't have to visit Him at His office. God travels extensively, so to cut down on His overhead He doesn't have an office.

All you have to do is know that God sent His son, Jesus Christ, to earth in order to save us and ask Jesus to come into your heart as your personal Saviour and Lord and to take control of your life. It is the old law of supply and demand. He goes where He is wanted. Include Him in all of your plans and He will be there on time.

If you wonder how He does it all, just remember that "with God, all things are possible." Effective time management helps too, I suppose, but whatever His method, there is no feeling more reassuring than knowing that God is watching out for you. The greatest Rhinoceros in the universe is on your side! He is your confidant, your associate, your advisor, your pal, your buddy, and He loves you.

READ HIS BOOK

God is really a character too. In order to better understand where He is coming from, you should read a book that He has out called "The Bible." I hear He is doing really well with it. He has found some good printers, set up some fantastic distribution channels, arranged for some financial backing, and it has

"God is your confidant, your associate, your advisor, your pal, your buddy, and He loves you."

been a consistent best-seller for thousands of years! It is tough to make it in the publishing field these days too, so He obviously knows the ropes. Read the Bible and pay particular attention to the story of Jesus Christ because if you know what Jesus is like, you will know what God is like. You will be proud to have Him as your safari guide.

Chapter 4

THE HUNT

Before you even begin your expedition through the jungle, you have to know what you are after. That makes sense, doesn't it? If you are out wandering around lost in the jungle, you are liable to become the hunted rather than the hunter. Don't let that happen to you. Know what you are hunting!

If you don't know what you are hunting, how do you know what kind of ammunition to bring? How do you know where to start looking if you don't even know what you are looking for? How will you ever know if you catch it? If you don't know what you are hunting, what the heck are you doing out in the jungle?

KEEP CHARGING OR BE EATEN ALIVE

You have to know what you are after or else the jungle will eat you up. If you don't keep moving, the quicksand will swallow you whole, two inch thick skin and all! Stay active. Keep those four legs of yours pounding the jungle ground blazing a trail through the thick foliage.

Know what you are after and keep after it relentlessly, tirelessly, and determinedly or else it will slip away from you through the underbrush and you are liable to lose it forever. You might lose sight of it for a while but NEVER, NEVER, NEVER quit charging at it. It is right around the next trail!

You might not hear it or smell it anymore, but keep charging at it anyway. It is there! It's in hiding, watching you come closer and closer, ready to flee when you get too close. But if you stop now, if you quit at this point when you are so close to catching it, it will laugh in your face and mock you.

PURE MOTIVATION

Know what you are after and never stop pursuing it until it is yours; never end the chase until you have gored it on your horn like a marshmallow on a stick. Keep the energy going. Do not let the cow disease, inertia, grind you to a stop or the jungle will consume you.

40

The jungle is characterized by energy and movement. It thrives on life and if you slow down the jungle will have no mercy on your useless frame of tired flesh and bones. The vultures, sensing weakness, will descend upon your body and finish you off. Keep your six thousand pounds moving at a good pace so that every living thing knows that you are a vital, functioning part of the jungle.

Finally, you have to know what you are after and keep pursuing it or the elements will turn your hunt into a disaster. Keep moving forward, never stop, or the jungle sun will bake your body draining any energy you have left right out of you. Keep charging and the breeze you create will keep you comfortable. Slow to a stop though and the bugs will rest in your eyes, the sun will make your skin burn, the birds of prey will greedily eye you, and the jungle will do its job to keep quitters out of its boundaries.

That sounds brutal, doesn't it? I don't want to make a nervous wreck out of you or make it hard for you to sleep at night for fear of a vulture pecking at your body or a gnat resting in your eye, but I have got to keep you charging. This is a motivational book. I'm trying to give you your money's worth.

YOU ARE ENJOYING YOURSELF

Of course, the most enjoyable part of hunting on a safari is the chase. Once you have

"You are a success if you are out there in the jungle on the trail of your goals."

caught what you are after, all the excitement is over. It's like climbing the highest mountain: climbing it is great fun, but what do you do when you get to the top? You can enjoy the view, but that gets old very quickly.

I remember as a kid driving in the car with my family to the Grand Canyon. Wow! It was fun . . . until we got there. The Grand Canyon gets to be as old as it looks within half an hour.

If you look back on some of your bigger accomplishments, you will recall the attaining of them as the exciting times. It is the events leading up to the kill that make the safari exciting. To go on a safari where the game is tied to a tree waiting for you to gun it down wouldn't be much fun, would it?

The saying that "success is a journey, not a destination" is absolutely true. You are a success if you are out there in the jungle on the trail of your goals. You may not realize it now unfortunately, but you are having the time of your life!

Chapter 5

QUIT YOUR JOB

A while back there was a television program on which they were asking kids the difference between work and play. Do you know the difference? This one obviously bright kid replied that "work is doing things that others think up for me to do, and play is doing things that I think up for me to do." Wasn't that a neat answer?

Of course, it would be unrealistic of me to suggest that everyone spend their lives doing "things that they think up for themselves to do." Some are going to have to spend their lives doing the unpleasant tasks and living a life of drudgery, right?

They are cows. Cows are as natural as death and disease. We wouldn't appreciate exciting, alive animals like rhinos if we didn't have cows to compare them to! Despite their unattractiveness and unappealing ways, we really do need cows.

COWS NEED SECURITY

Cows are the only ones willing to trade their freedom for a regular paycheck. They thrive on working for others because they need direction, they need to be led and they survive by having others care for them. Give a cow a regular income, a few paid holidays per year, medical benefits, maybe throw in a little life insurance and a cow will give you its life!

You see, cows are good for something because who else would do that for you? Cows have been conveniently brainwashed that they must work for a living! They don't know that they have a choice. When you are doing what you enjoy doing, it is not work. Why spend your life doing something unpleasant?

THE ENTREPRENEUR VS. THE SUPERCOW

In the jungle, you can either be the one who does what others think up for you to do, or you can be the one thinking up things for others to do. The latter is the job of the entrepreneur. Being an entrepreneur is the most rewarding, most enjoyable, and most exciting position in the jungle.

But how many kids have you heard say they want to be an entrepreneur when they grow up? Very, very few, I am sure. I never even heard the word "entrepreneur" until I was well out of high school because the public schools are set up and run by the government which is the biggest cow pasture in the United Jungles of America. In fact, cows that work for the government are no ordinary cows. They are supercows!

At least the cows that work in private enterprise help create a product or service that benefits all the animals in the jungle. These cows work with some competition and REALLY DO WORK because if they don't work, they get kicked out of the pasture. That is not the case with government supercows.

ALL ANIMALS ARE NOT CREATED EQUAL

Supercows are an extremely ugly and disgusting breed of cow because they produce absolutely nothing while robbing from the jungle population to pay for their bureaucratic empires which regulate and interfere in the lives of all animals. Can you see why it would not be in this contemptible animal's best interests to teach young animals about the opportunities of our free enterprise system and encourage the young entrepreneur?

"The bureaucratic supercow is the worst breed of cow there is."

Rhinoceros entrepreneurs worry the supercows. After all, the supercow's only purpose in life is to shackle and restrain, to "protect" and to rule over, and attempt to create equality in an unequal jungle. Equal rights are what we want, not trying to make all animals equal. Everything the supercow stands for goes against the moral fiber of the entrepreneur. Unfortunately, regular cows encourage the proliferation and activity of the supercows because, naturally, most cow's dreams are to be supercows. Being a supercow means better security, more pay, additional benefits, and less work.

But as more and more rhinos become fed up with the parasitic supercows, the supercow's existence is being challenged. As a matter of fact, we are now experiencing the beginnings of the Rhinocerotic Revolution in which the supercows are going to be reduced to mere cows. We will get to that in a later chapter.

DO YOU ENJOY YOUR WORK?

If this chapter has upset you, please bear with me because there are always exceptions. First of all, let me clarify my views regarding work. Just because someone has a job working for someone else does not automatically qualify him or her as a cow. Some animals really enjoy their work. Some find it fascinating and could not be happier. Some would perhaps even pay for the privilege of doing what they are doing. Hey, if that is the position you are in, that is great! Keep charging!

But if you spend five days a week doing something that is boring, that you do not enjoy, that makes your life miserable, then I am sorry, but you are a cow! A true rhino would not waste his life that way! No one has you in an arm lock! You are not tethered to a tree! You don't need permission to go to the bathroom! You have the power to choose and you are living in a jungle where you still have the freedom to exercise that choice. If you don't enjoy what you are doing every day, *WHY* are you doing it? Because you are a cow, that's why! You are a thin-skinned, snivelling, cowardly, cowering cow!

Don't let me hurt your feelings, but DO try to get upset because maybe if you get mad enough, maybe if the embarrassment or anger makes your blood start flowing, maybe if you get disgusted enough with being a cow you will take action. You might even quit! Go ahead!

ONE WALL PER FORKLIFT PLEASE

I remember one of the first jobs that I ever quit. Right after finishing high school, I worked at a computer company in the receiving department. My job was to unload the trucks and process all the incoming material. I drove a forklift which was fun. While learning to operate it, I drove it right through a wall which was exciting. You are only allowed to drive a forklift through a wall once though, so the excitement of driving it soon wore off.

Being a developing rhinoceros, I looked for new territory to charge in and was promoted to the stock room after six months in receiving. Two months after that, I was promoted to expeditor. Now, if there was ever a position designed to promote nervous breakdowns it is the job of the expeditor. The expeditor's function is, logically, to expedite.

I was in charge of seeing that production flowed smoothly from the receiving department to the stock room, on to the assembly floor, to the testing department, back to the re-work department and then, hopefully, to shipping. The first thing I learned is that production NEVER flows smoothly. One of my bigger challenges while running between manufacturing locations was chasing down what we called "shortages." There was only one thing that we were never short on and that was shortages.

Naturally, everyone in the company hates the expeditor. I had to be constantly needling and begging, finagling and demanding work through the production floor in order to meet the deadlines. When the computers weren't out in time, you know whose fault it was.

One day I broke down. At the time, I was sharing an office with another thick-skinned expeditor whose skin happened to be much thicker than mine was at that time. Our desks were piled high with "Rush" orders and reports of part shortages, the phones were ringing constantly with nothing but problems, we were both working 10 to 12 hours a day, and suddenly the impossibility of it all overcame me. I just laid my head on my desk and started sobbing uncontrollably, competing with the ringing of the telephone. I don't recall what my buddy said to calm me down. Maybe it was something like, "Don't be such a cow, Scott!"

MY FIRST BUSINESS

I recovered to continue the grind and then I met Kim. After a few months' acquaintance, I found out that Kim could clip dogs. Being a budding entrepreneur, I took advantage of the situation and I made Kim my girlfriend. Wow! This was great! Now I had a girlfriend that could clip poodles!

My next move was to suggest that we start our own business—maybe a dog grooming parlor! Great! This was my chance to quit my expediting job and put Kim to work! I told Kim

"You are only allowed to drive a forklift through a wall once, so the excitement of driving it soon wore off."

that we would call it "Kim's Grooming" and that clinched the deal.

Monday, I went in to work and I gave my two week notice. What an exhilarating feeling! My supervisor sat down with me and told me what a fantastic future I could have if I stayed with the company. He told me that soon I would be promoted to production planner. When he heard my plans to start a dog grooming shop, he really tried to convince me to stay, but I was adamant and in two weeks I would have my freedom.

And so Kim's Grooming was born. This was my first exposure to the science of motivation because I had to do something, right? I couldn't clip the dogs! Besides, I soon discovered that the number of dogs that Kim clipped was directly related to how much money I was going to make. But we only charged six dollars a dog and Kim was such a perfectionist that she could only finish three dogs a day, no matter how much I attempted to motivate her.

MY FIRST BUSINESS FAILS

After six months, our business had gone to the dogs. I was out of money, Kim was out of desire to clip poodles, and I found myself back at the computer company asking my supervisor for my job back. I told him that I recognized the errors of my ways, that I really was better off with them, and that I never wanted to see another poodle as long as I lived. And I meant it . . . the part about not seeing another poodle!

The next week I was Mr. Expeditor again, only this time it was worse, for now I had experienced real freedom and the joys of being my own boss. My entrepreneurial addiction had taken root. I had experienced steak and everyone else was chewing on hamburger! I had felt heaven and everyone else had only ever known hell! I HAD TO get out again!

I GET TO TASTE STEAK AGAIN

Then another idea came to me to start a mobile auto wash business. That's what I would do! I would install water tanks, pumps and hoses in the back of my truck and wash executives' cars in the parking lots at their offices. I told a few friends about it at work and they let me know that it was a stupid idea.

"How are you going to wash cars in the sun without getting water spots?" they demanded. "No one will pay five dollars to have you wash their car! You can't get soap on the parking lot! You can't do it because you will get water on the other cars! There is a water shortage and the city won't let you do it. It will never work!"

I quit telling my friends about it and on Monday morning I went in to tell my supervisor that I was leaving again. This time he didn't tell me what a marvelous future I had there. Rather disgustedly, he told me that I would never be able to come back and get a job with that company. This was the end! That suited me fine and in two weeks I was free again.

IN SEARCH OF CAPITAL

Now I had to borrow some money. I drove down to the bank where I had paid off a loan for my truck. They had sent me a form letter urging me to always borrow money from them. Sure thing! I anticipated no trouble in securing the needed funds.

Confidently, I strode into the bank and told the loan officer all about my new mobile auto wash plans and asked about getting some money to get it all going. The banker tightened up, leaned back in his chair and asked me if I could give him a statement.

I said, "Sure . . . I'm very optimistic!"

Apparently that wasn't the kind of statement the banker was looking for because I didn't get the loan. After three more banks turned me down, I started to get nervous. I'm telling you, if you ever have to have a heart transplant, ask for the heart of a banker because they don't get used very much.

"Maybe I should have taken care of this detail before I quit my job," I began to think. At this time I was 20 years old and still living with my parents. I did not tell them that I had quit my job for fear that they would disown me. So, every morning I got up as usual and left the house as if I was going to work. A week went by and it was clear that no bank was going to lend me any money. In desperation, I drove to my grandparents' house and told them the whole story. I got the money . . . $500.

I MARRIED A RHINO

The next three years were very exciting. Kim and I married and went to Australia for a month on our honeymoon. We came back and ran the mobile auto wash together. Only this time, Kim did the motivating and I did the work.

Within a year, we had two trucks and two full routes. I hired my younger brother, Gregg, to help me, and together we started making a lot of money. We were eventually charging (no pun intended) $15 per wash and we had everyone on a weekly schedule. Business got better and then we hired Kim's younger brother, Larry, to start another route. By this time, we had been featured in the papers, and a national magazine did a little story on us. Then I was interviewed on television and the business was even mentioned in a couple of books. We were flying—and they said that it would never work!

Looking back now, I shudder to think that if I didn't have the audacity to quit, I might still be an expeditor! *If you hate your job,* either look for another one or start your own business. Just get out!

DON'T CONTRIBUTE TO THE BUREAUCRACY

Finally, I realize that there are undoubtedly many exceptions to the rule that anyone who works for the government is a supercow. Probably the biggest exceptions would be those serving in the military services (Army, Navy, Air Force, Marines, etc.) or protection such as police services. The government does have a role there. It's the regulating bureaucracy that we don't want or need. If you work for the bureaucracy, one of the best things you could ever do for the United Jungles of America would be to quit and get a job in private enterprise, or to start your own business. In this way, you would be helping to create products or services that we animals want, not services that are forced upon us.

Chapter 6

THE FEAR OF
BEING SQUISHED

Being a rhino means being self-motivated. Now, there is quite a difference between self-motivation and just plain, old motivation. First of all, what exactly is motivation? Well, the dictionary says that "motivation" is *"the condition of being motivated."* That is a typical dictionary definition: it doesn't tell you anything. O.K., let's play their game then. What does "being motivated" mean? The dictionary says that "motivate" means *"to provide with a motive."* We're getting closer. Well then, dear dictionary, what is a "motive?" Now here comes the meaty part. This is what becoming a success boils down to. A motive is *"some-*

thing that causes a person to act." Of course, by "person" they mean a "rhinoceros." That is undoubtedly a typographical error which will hopefully be corrected in their next printing.

Therefore, *motivation* is providing yourself with something that is going to cause you to take action. The following story illustrates how most everyone is motivated.

LITTLE GREEN FROG STORY

It seems that a little green frog had fallen into a rut in a road and could not quite jump high enough to get himself out. His frog buddies were at the top of the ditch urging him on.

"Come on! You can do it!" they would all yell in unison at the top of their frog lungs. The little frog would jump as hard as he could, but he just could not jump high enough, despite everyone's encouragement and advice. After two hours, the frog was still in the rut and his buddies could wait for him no longer. They went hopping away without him.

Later in the day, just as they were getting ready to swim in the lake and do some croaking, the frogs saw their little buddy who had been trapped in the rut. Figuring that he would never get out of there, they excitedly exclaimed, "What happened? How did you get out of the rut?" The frog turned to them and said, "A big truck came down the road and I HAD to get out!"

DON'T GET SQUISHED

It was the fear of being squished that caused the frog to take action! If you think for a moment, isn't that how most everyone, especially a cow, is motivated? It is the fear of being squished! In school, the kids do their homework and study for the tests to avoid failing. In this case, an "F" is getting squished.

When these kids leave school, they get a job to earn money. The motivation here is the fear of starvation, and they work just hard enough to keep from being fired, which is another form of squishing. If you analyze why most animals do anything, it will usually come down to the fear of being squished.

Now, I am not saying that that is undesirable. Often times, that is what is needed to get out of a rut. A businessman who fears the prospect of bankruptcy is going to be motivated, isn't he? If he doesn't get going on something, he is going to be actively involved in a major squish . . . his own!

My point is: what is going to motivate that frog now that he is out of the rut and the danger of being squished is gone? Now the frog is in the lake taking it easy. Remember the cow disease, inertia? The tendency for all objects, including us, is to remain still. That is a scientific fact. Once the danger of being squished, which originally caused us to take action, is gone, our tendency is to stop taking action and do nothing.

BE A SQUISHER, NOT A SQUISHEE

Right here is where the rhinos are separated from the cows, because the rhinos are SELF-MOTIVATED. They KEEP ON GOING! Why wait around to get squished again? That is a terrible way to go through life! That sort of motivation can give you restless nights. Better to be self-motivated and far exceed that point where the fear of being squished is your impetus to action.

Therefore, you need to provide yourself with an incentive to keep charging. Rhinoceroses don't do just enough to get by like the cows do. Whatever rhinos do, they go all out, full steam ahead, and damn-the-torpedoes!

What is going to cause you to do that kind of charging? Do you have a good enough reason? You *know* that if you don't take action, there is ABSOLUTELY NO HOPE for you! Don't be like the horse who could hit the ball but didn't run! You have *got to* take action! You don't have a choice. It is right there in the dictionary. Look it up for yourself if you don't believe me.

IS THERE A DOCTOR IN THE HOUSE?

Undoubtedly, there will be times when your motors start to slow down. You will lose interest in your projects and your energy will drop off to a dangerous level. Sitting around the house watching television and eating Danish pastry will sound very appealing to you and you might even permit yourself to engage in such decadence.

Watch out! The cow disease, inertia, has entered your blood stream either by associating with cows, or you might have picked it up off a dirty toilet seat in some gas station somewhere. Now you are at a critical stage. The inertia is capable of invading your whole body and reducing you to a bovine state, unless you can fight it with your indomitable rhinoceros spirit.

If you find yourself with a bad case of inertia, where it is almost too much of a hassle to read this book, let alone do anything else, and there is no Doctor of Rhinocerology present, listen to me. Do you actually want to be a cow? Do you enjoy losing and lying around in your manure? Is it your idea of fun to decay and putrefy like a pile of unsightly rubbish? Cows are as low down as you can get. They are lower than whale droppings! Do you want to be that low?

Or do you want to be a rhinoceros exploding with energy living a happy, useful, exciting, and productive life? Do you want the blood to pump through your body again and enrich all your cells and bring them back to life? Do you want to live and try or do you want to quit and die?

INVEST SOME ENERGY IN YOURSELF

If the idea of being a cow thoroughly disgusts you, TAKE ACTION NOW or the inertia will drop you again. If you have nothing else to do, put on your shorts and running shoes and go for a run. Just start running! Spending energy creates more energy. You have got to get steamed up to have steam. Laziness and energy are the two opposites. Like oil and water, they do not mix. Like fire and water, they can destroy each other. Burn your oil!

Whew! That was close, huh? We almost lost you! How do you feel now? Your horn was starting to droop, you were losing weight quickly and your skin was looking thin in spots. The best thing for you now is plenty of fluids and NO REST. WHEN YOU'RE HOT, DON'T STOP! Keep the fire raging and your oil burning. Keep charging!

MOTIVATIONAL CHEMISTRY

The best way to keep your fire lit and your engines humming is to use the same emotions that kept you from being squished. Anger, fear, and embarrassment are very powerful emotions which will get you going. Think for a moment about the changes your body undergoes when you get *really* mad. Your brain sends a hormone called noradrenalin through your body which causes your heart to start beating faster. You start to breathe at a quicker pace. Your pupils enlarge and your digestion stops. You are now ready for action! When you are in this condition, you don't lie down and fall asleep. You feel like knocking down a wall. But instead of doing that, use your sudden surge of strength to your advantage to help propel you forward.

YOUR BEST REVENGE

When I was building up my mobile auto wash business, a driving force for me were the cows who told me that it would never work. Their mockery was my motivation. I think it was Frank Sinatra who said that "The best revenge is massive success."

To take advantage of this form of motivation, keep a "despite list." You are going to succeed, you are going to triumph, you are going to prevail DESPITE these cows. Assemble a list of everyone who doubts what you say you are going to do, everyone who laughs at your plans, anyone who questions your abilities, and then do what you said you were going to do and leave them choking in

"If you have nothing else to do, put on your running gear and go for a run."

your dust. Get so far ahead of them that they are left in a state of bewilderment and then forget them. They are only cows.

Wow! I must sound like a really vicious animal. Actually, I am a lovable guy. It's just that, like Steve Martin might say, "Motivation is not pretty."

Chapter 7

THE FREE
ENTERPRISE GAME

Life in the jungle can either be a game or a battle. It is your choice. Which would you rather participate in? Personally, I would rather be involved in a game than a bloody battle. Actually, it is just the way you look at it. All of us, whether we are cows or magnificent rhinoceroses, have to play by the same rules. Here in the United Jungles of America, we play the free enterprise game which runs on the capitalistic system using money.

Of course, money is only a "medium of exchange." In itself, money is absolutely worthless. It is the goods and services that it represents that give it value. We could have used chickens instead of dollars, but it would have

"We could have used chickens instead of dollars, but it would have been awkward in certain situations."

been awkward in certain situations. To come by this medium of exchange you have to know the basic rule of the free enterprise game which is simply: *You must give to get.* There really is no free lunch, contrary to what the government would have you believe.

It is this simple system of private enterprise that has built our great jungle. Americans enjoy a personal freedom that is not found anywhere else in the world. Yet there are supercows out there who would have us reduced to a bovine welfare state if they had their way. It is our duty as rhinoceroses to see that these cows are kept in their place. We owe it to our founding rhinos and to the future rhinos of America to see that our government is restrained or else it will grow larger and more expensive and continue to interfere in the private and business affairs of all of us.

THE GOVERNMENT IS YOUR ENEMY

The only enemy of a rhinoceros is a bloated, all-powerful government which threatens our freedom. Our best strategy is to ignore the government. Have as little to do with it as possible. It is the cows who are constantly turning to government to solve their problems, to feed and clothe them and ask for help for all their special interests that encourage government to do things that our founding rhinos never intended it to do. In this way, government suffocates freedom. Rhinos need the freedom of the jungle to charge in. Let's NEVER let them pen us into the false security of a manure-filled pasture with the cows.

BE PREPARED TO BE EXPLOITED

You will occasionally hear from some professional supercow who will tell you that the wealthy accumulate wealth by exploiting the poor. Isn't that the most absolutely asinine statement you have ever heard? If you understand the one rule of the free enterprise game—YOU MUST GIVE TO GET—you can see that it is the ones who choose not to play the game (the complaining poor) who exploit those of us who do (the wealthy producers). The poor have nothing to exploit! It is the contributors, the wealthy, who pay the taxes that give the poor their welfare payments. That is exploitation!

The poor continue to exploit the wealthy who risk capital and energy to start businesses giving others jobs. The producers build hospitals, shopping centers, libraries, parks and everything else that makes life more enjoyable. These are all for the poor to exploit.

DO YOUR OWN EXPLOITING

Know your jungle. The better you understand your world and how it works, the better you are going to be at exploiting it. Know where the watering holes are so that you won't die of thirst. Know the densest part of the jungles where you can seek rest. Even rhinos have to take a breather once in a while. Know which animals live in which part of the jungle and which are friendly to rhinoceroses. Know where the nicest, most lush part of the jungle is so that you can make your home there. Rhinos do not live in the barren, dry desert. (Unless there is a private water hole, of course). Make sure that you are where you belong.

Know the jungle so that you can take advantage of it. Your concrete jungle consists of freeways, thousands of businesses offering a myriad of products and services, millions of animals with money to buy and millions of animals wanting to work. The rhino entrepreneur's task is to give those unemployed animals something to work at and to give those money-laden animals something to purchase.

College educated animals depend heavily on entrepreneurially inclined rhinoceroses. Someone has to build the hospitals for the doctors to practice in. Someone has to build businesses and corporations to give lawyers and executives something to do. Someone has to build up this jungle creating more good for all, so that the intellectual, liberal supercows will have something to criticize and complain about. If we don't build it up, who will?

YOU WERE BORN WITH A HORN

We know what being a rhinoceros stands for. The rhinos are the producers, the movers and shakers, the ones responsible for the world's progress. We've got quite a responsibility, don't we? If it were not for us rhinos, the world would be in a pretty sorry state, wouldn't it? Imagine if the cows held the reins on the world. We would be up to our necks in manure!

Throughout history, there have always been rhinos and there have always been cows. That has never changed and it never will change. Just be thankful that you are one of the rhinos! When you wake up in the morning, be thankful that you were not born with bells around your neck and the first sound you made was not "moooo."

You were born a rhinoceros! The first sound you made was a screaming, high-pitched rhino roar! The doctor didn't have to slap your bottom to get you going. You were born motivated! You paid the bill and got out of there! You had to get out into the jungle and get your horns into something right away.

"You were born a rhinoceros! The doctor didn't have to slap your bottom to get you going."

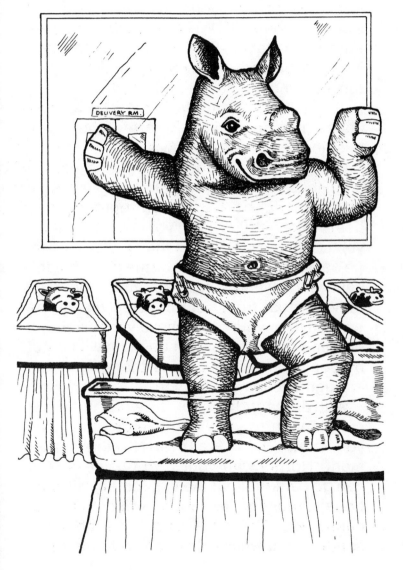

BUSINESS CAN BE HABIT-FORMING

Do you have your own business started? There is nothing wrong in working for others if you enjoy it, but if you don't enjoy it, why not work for yourself? We are playing the free enterprise game! Don't you want to play? Nothing matches the excitement and adventure of being an entrepreneur. I am convinced that there would be less drug and alcohol abuse if more animals started their own businesses.

Look at it this way: taking drugs and starting a business both involve risk, right? In fact, if you want to be daring, entrepreneurship beats taking drugs. With your own business, you could be sued for all that you are worth, go bankrupt, be harassed by the government, have employees steal from you, have customers steal from you, develop ulcers, be evicted from your office, have your inventory become obsolete, or just be plain wiped out by your competition. Does that sound like enough excitement for you?

With drugs and alcohol, the worst thing that can happen to you is an overdose causing your death. Then it is all over! No more excitement! Not so with your own business. You can go bankrupt but the excitement will continue. Creditors, like devils, will continue to haunt you. The government will continue sending you their collection of forms to fill out. A lawsuit could last for years! You see, business is risky stuff. Drugs do not even compare!

Maybe kids take drugs to feel good. Well, how good can turning your brain and body to mush feel? Running your own business, on the other hand, stimulates your nerve endings rather than deaden them. There is nothing like the rush of excitement from creating something from nothing.

Drugs cannot give you the euphoric feelings of accomplishment, of taking on a challenge and succeeding, of pitting yourself against the elements of the jungle where survival of the fittest is the rule and winning. Wow! Once you have had the slightest taste of victory in the jungle, you are hooked. You will never be able to work for anyone else again.

Finally, drugs cost you money while your own business can make you money! With your own business, you get all the benefits of being daring and feeling good, and on top of all that, you are liable to become wealthy doing it! Become entrepreneurially addicted!

BLOW YOUR MIND

In time, your small business habit may not satisfy you. You will crave more excitement, more risk, more stimulation, and you will start to experiment with more daring forms of business. Peer pressure may get you involved

"More of your time will be spent hanging around undesirable characters in the jungle like lawyers and accountants."

in incorporating. More of your time will be spent hanging around undesirable characters in the jungle like lawyers and accountants. Before you know what has happened, you will be investing in real estate projects and various other tax shelters.

Vast expanses of land will become developed under your control, your enterprise will employ thousands of animals as your bank account swells and your mother will wonder where she went wrong. YOU ARE HOOKED! You are an entrepreneur! ADMIT IT! That is the first step toward making sure that you STAY that way. The jungle is yours to exploit. You would never go back to working for anyone else once you realize that. Sorry, Mom.

Chapter 8

AN ENTREPRENEURIAL SAFARI

You have decided to venture out on your own through the jungle. Congratulations! I hope your primary reason is not for money. Money is too smart for that. The minute it sees you coming, it is gone. Your safari will be frustrating and unsatisfying.

Go, instead, for fun. Go to see just what you can do and to have the time of your life! Enjoy the hunt, take pleasure in the scenery and you will catch the money unaware. If you go just for money, you are liable to get into something that you don't particularly enjoy . . . like grooming dogs.

I chose the publishing field because I enjoy writing. The art of promotion and publicity also intrigues me and it gives me opportunities to speak before groups which I also like. If I don't make a million dollars, it won't matter because I will have fun. I would rather be happy and broke than wealthy and miserable, if those were the only choices available. Of course, those aren't the only choices. Being happy and wealthy is the best way to go and if you start out with something that you enjoy, the money will come to you.

NECESSARY INGREDIENTS

There are three basic elements which make up the entrepreneurial safari. It is these three ingredients which allow the capitalistic system to run so successfully and if you can learn to skillfully combine these three elements, you are capable of great things. They are *money, energy,* and *ideas.* Virtually all the great inventions, accomplishments, and products have come about through the proficient use of these three ingredients. They can work together to build successful businesses, create great wealth, and, applied correctly, they can make your life extremely enjoyable.

LACK OF "RHINO" IS THE ROOT OF ALL EVIL

Money is by far the most powerful of the three ingredients. If you have a lot of money, you can always buy the energy and ideas of others. Incidentally, did you know that the word "rhino" also means "money?" It is true! Look it up in your dictionary if you don't believe me!

If you don't have enough "rhino," don't worry about it. Of the three ingredients, money is the only one that is not natural. Everyone is born with energy and ideas but no one is born with money. Just as money can buy energy and ideas, so too can good ideas and properly directed energy secure money.

HAVE HAPPY ENERGY

Energy is another important requirement for a successful entrepreneurial safari. Energy is most conveniently obtained by doing what you enjoy. If you love what you are doing, naturally you are going to have the energy to do it. When you go skiing, do you lie in bed in the morning dreading getting up and having to go ski down those stupid mountains? Of course not! You are in line for your lift ticket before they are even open! And do you quit early and come in before the lift shuts down? Heck no! You race up and down trying to get in as many runs as you can. Then you can't wait until tomorrow! That is the way you have to run your business in order to succeed, so make sure that you are in a field that interests you.

Finally, you must have good ideas. Everything that exists today was once just an idea. Who knows what could exist a year from now because of an idea you might come up with! If you can think, you can imagine. And if you can imagine, then you are creative!

Don't forget that money is just an idea. It has no tangible value. Money merely represents goods and services. That was a good idea, wasn't it? With your own brilliant ideas, you can devise means of getting some of that worthless paper. You might as well. What else are you doing that is so important that it can't wait? As long as you are here, why not enjoy yourself and play the game?

THE REAL WINNERS

Money can be used to keep score although the real winners are those who had fun capturing the money. Without a doubt, you will have lots of money, if you don't already. You have ideas and energy which will allow you to get your first wad of "rhino" and then you will combine that money to create more money. The cycle will continue until you are fabulously wealthy. Then you have to remember to keep it all in the proper perspective.

God told us not to lay up treasures on earth because He knew that they wouldn't last. He said that the moths and rust would consume it, and thieves would break in and steal. How did He know that? That is exactly what happens and if you're not expecting it, you can become very frustrated.

TAKE A WALK ON THE BOARDWALK

Keep in mind that your thriving business and all of your material possessions are merely temporary pieces in the game of life. It is a lot like playing Monopoly. You could be putting hotels on all of your properties, you could own all of the railroads and then everyone playing might decide that it is late and they better go home because they have got to get up early in the morning.

All the play money is put back into the "bank," the title deeds are gathered up, and all the houses and hotels are dumped back into the box. The game is over. How would you feel? GREAT! Because you were winning! You knew that the game would eventually end but that didn't stop you from playing to win. How would you have felt had you been losing? What if you had landed on Boardwalk owned by someone else and it had a hotel on it? You would have been the one who suggested that it was getting late!

Sure, it was temporary. But that doesn't mean you shouldn't try. Temporary winning is always better than temporary losing. You could spend your lifetime on your entrepreneurial safari building a large estate and then get hit by the torpedo that has your name on it. But that's all right. You were winning and living a productive life. Better that, than to live a losing life and actually look forward to getting hit by the big torpedo.

When you go to Hawaii for a vacation, you don't sit in your hotel room and mope because you know that the vacation can't last forever. You get out on the beach and enjoy the time that you do have there.

REDISTRIBUTION OF A MERCEDES

God said that thieves would break in and steal, so if your brand new, diesel Mercedes is stolen, don't worry about it. You can get another one! Better to have independent thieves get it from you anyway, than to have the government supercows expropriate it.

At least the thieves have to work to get it. The government would just tax it right away from you. At least the thieves would enjoy the fruits of their labor. The government would try to redistribute it. At least the thieves would make money from the theft, while the government would lose money paying for the redistribution. Let the thieves take it! You were tired of the color, anyway.

Enjoy your material rewards here on earth while you have them, but remember that it is all temporary. Your real treasure is in heaven, when the game is all over here. But go up as a winner, not a loser!

Chapter 9

THE RHINOCEROTIC REVOLUTION

Watch out supercows! We rhinos have had your bleeding heart politics long enough! Your growing pastures are creating an uneasy stir among those in the jungle. The rules and regulations that you spew out are straining the tolerance of all animals to yield to such submission. Even some cows are now questioning the benefits of having Big Brother Cow governing their lives. The following letter from Linda Timmons to the "Los Angeles Times" on February 22, 1979 expresses the feelings of many.

I've got the paycheck blues again, and it made me start thinking about America, land of the free. I had always interpreted that phrase to mean I was free to live my life the way I chose. I believed I had the right to make all decisions affecting my life as long as I didn't harm anyone or break any laws. I believed that the laws were there to protect me, and that people who broke them were criminals.

These concepts always sounded fine to me. I was sure I could live a happy, productive life within their framework, because I knew I was an honest, conscientious person responsible for my actions. I was proud to be an American.

I lived with this fantasy until I was 19 years old. That was when my husband received his draft notice, on our first wedding anniversary. Within days, the boy I loved since I was 13 was gone. The government, which made the laws to "protect" me, said that he had to go where it sent him, and that he had to do what it ordered. If he didn't, he would be a criminal and could go to jail. And so they sent him to Vietnam. They risked his life without his consent. I didn't understand.

My husband came back safely after 11 months, and was honorably discharged from the service. We started a family, saved our money and bought a small house in Hermosa Beach, where we'd grown up. We were careful not to get into debt. Each year the property taxes on our small house increased; in 1976 they doubled, and then last year they doubled again. We couldn't afford the $2,400 that the government wanted—but this was our home, this was the town where we grew up. What were we to do? The government, which made laws to protect us, said that we had to pay if we wanted to stay. I didn't understand.

Proposition 13 lowered our property taxes, so that we could keep our home. But now the court is suggesting that soon my children may not be able to attend the school at the end of our street; they might have to ride a schoolbus for up to 40 minutes each way, to go to school in someone else's town. We chose to live in this town because we grew up here. It is a small community, with lots of involved citizens. We wanted our children to have pride in their neighborhood, and in its school. The government which makes rules to protect us, says that this is not important; something called integration (not education) is more important.

Receiving what's left after taxes of my first few paychecks of 1979 has prompted me to reflect on my life. I believe that I finally understand: I am not free at all; it is the government that's free to do what it wants. The laws are not designed to protect my family and me; they are designed to protect the government. And we, the people, support this system with our money, our children—our very lives. If we don't, we risk breaking the law.

Yes, now I understand, and I am not so sure how I feel anymore about being an honest, conscientious person responsible for my actions. America, land of the free—it rings hollow. I'm still proud to be an American, and I wouldn't want to live anywhere else, but I am not as naive as I once was.

The rebellion has begun! President Reagan's landslide victory over Jimmy Carter in 1980 signaled the new beginning. The message from the jungle is clear: get rid of the super-cows! Rhino Ronald Reagan was the first president elected in a long time who promised the jungle population less ... less government, less regulation and lower taxes!

THE BASICS OF REBELLION

Let's go back twenty years to the decade of the 60's. Remember the hippies? Young animals growing up then were rebelling against the system. Now, there's nothing wrong in protesting, right? Rebellion is a natural part of growing up. The hard part is finding something to protest and the easiest targets to attack are whatever your parents believe in. Parents are never with it, you know.

Back in the 60's the parents didn't believe in free love, so that was a natural! Parents believed that only girls should have long hair, so all of a sudden, the guys had to have it. No parents wanted their children to smoke marijuana, so naturally it became very popular. You get the idea. Whatever your parents *want* you to do, you *don't want* to do and whatever they *don't want* you to do you *really want* to do. That's rebellion in a nutshell.

DON'T TRUST ANYONE OVER 30!

Now look at what has happened. The flower children, the hippies and the yippies of the sixties are now reaching parental age. A lot of them are even over 30 years old! Remember that we kids do not trust anyone over 30!

These children of the sixties are now taking over the system and gaining power where before they had none. You can find them teaching their liberal views in school now, there are many voicing their opinions in books, in the papers, on television and in the movies. Hundreds of thousands of them are working for the government, some aiming for positions of power to ensure that we live the way they believe we should live. Their goal seems to be to make life for everyone risk free and easy. They push for gun control, busing, equality, minimum wage laws, free school lunches, more welfare, no nuclear energy plants, seat belt laws and so on.

NEW WAVE OF DISCONTENT

But guess what? The children of the 60's are now the parents, and the children of the 80's are beginning to rebel. Compare the punkers of today with the hippies of the 60's. The hippies wore long, sloppy hair and beards. Now the style is very short hair sometimes with streaks of bright colors, and absolutely no facial hair. Where the hippies wore flared leg jeans, the punkers wear straight leg pants. Hippies sang about free love and peace. New wave music of today is loaded with violence. The mellow drugs of the 60's are being replaced with the more violent and dangerous drugs such as PCP or, the trend now is to use no drugs at all.

There is a definite upheaval occurring. It is the rhinocerotic revolution and it is quickly changing the ways of the jungle. The liberalism of the 60's is now surrendering to Reagan's conservatism which will soon merge with the libertarianism of the 80's and the 90's.

LAISSEZ-FAIRE FREE ENTERPRISE

Rather than fighting for cradle to grave security like the old generation, the new generation will battle for a laissez-faire form of capitalism. Laissez-faire means "a doctrine opposing governmental interference in economic affairs *beyond* the minimum necessary for the maintenance of peace and property rights." In other words, the new generation will want NO government at all, except to protect the lives and property of all the animals in the United Jungles of America.

That may sound shocking to you now and that is why the young generation will fight for it. Long hair on males used to be shocking. Marijuana used to be shocking. The Beatles used to be shocking. Don't forget the basics of rebelling: whatever *they* don't want, *we* want, and vice versa.

RHINOCEROTIC OPPORTUNITIES

Another reason for the drive toward laissez-faire capitalism is the fact that there will be tremendous new opportunities opening up during the rhinocerotic revolution and no one will want any supercows slowing things down with their regulations. Fantastic new technologies are now emerging with the promise of new fortunes to be made and no one is going to be willing to be taxed to the hilt in order to pay for any encumbered bureau-cracies.

The fortunes made by rhinos such as J. Paul Getty in oil during the early part of this century are going to be duplicated, but not in oil. Oil, gas, and coal are on their way out because we are running out! No one thought to pump any oil back into the ground, so now it is becoming harder to find. And the bureau-cratic blunderers have wrapped the entire industry with red tape and regulations that make the exploration of new sources of oil prohibitively expensive or impossible.

Just to show you how the supercows think —did you know that the bureaucrats have established a Department of Energy with approximately 20,000 employees which has never produced one kilowatt of energy? Not even one drop of oil! All they have ever done is restrict the production and distribution of oil, a noble goal for a government agency. Hey, forget it! Oil will soon be obsolete any-way. Fortunately, so will the government!

As new, more efficient sources of energy are developed, do you think we are going to let the supercows get their hooves into it and jumble things up again? No way! If there is going to be any agency set up, it will be a Department of Bureaucracy whose purpose will be to restrict the production and distribution of supercows! Think of all the money that agency could save us!

The future is in energy sources that are non-exhaustible and produce no pollution. The great race is on to find and develop new energy for the jungle! You could be a part of it and make millions of dollars! Watch for solar technology, geothermal, and hydrogen developments. Everything is being tried now as the frantic race gets under way. Wave power, coconut waste, and even burning cow crackers is being attempted to provide an energy source that will not run out on us.

NUCLEAR HANDBALL COURTS

Nuclear technology is not going to make it as a primary energy source either, for three reasons. Number one is that the government helped initiate it which tells you right away that we probably don't need it.

Secondly, conventional reactors rely on uranium and what happens when we run out of uranium? I have never actually been inside a nuclear reactor, but from the outside they look like they would make neat handball courts!

Thirdly, they produce waste which is inefficient. The new energy sources will create no waste or will use what waste they do create to produce more energy. However, any potential danger or risk of nuclear energy

"I have never actually been inside a nuclear reactor, but from the outside they look like they would make neat handball courts."

is NOT a reason for ruling it out. Life in the jungle will always be risky. The cows just can't seem to get that through their heads. In fact, if the continuance of nuclear technology will help the government protect our freedom from wild animals, which is all they were originally set up to do, I'm all for it.

Obviously, the Russians aren't interested in slowing down their nuclear growth. We want to get rid of the government messing around with our lives, but let's not let the Russians do it for us! We need nuclear technology as a deterrent to aggression against our United Jungles, but let's look for other sources of energy to run our electric horn massagers and power our lawnmowers. We have got to keep the grass short to avoid luring any cows who might think that they have found a pasture.

THE COMPUTERIZED JUNGLE

Where Henry Ford made his fortune in cars, rhinos of the rhinocerotic revolution will be amassing great wealth through the proliferation of the computer. In 1979, according to "Computerworld" magazine, "If the auto industry had done what the computer industry has done in the last 30 years, a Rolls-Royce would cost $2.50 and get 2,000,000 miles to the gallon."

Soon every home in the jungle will have a computer! They will be as common as toilets! Can you imagine the money that is going to be made in this industry? It is exciting! Many fortunes are going to be made in the development, the manufacture, the distribution, the repair, and the sales of home computers.

The decade of the computer entrepreneur is here as the electronics industry invades the jungle. Your car may soon be able to talk to you and you will communicate with the outside world through your computer terminal, which could eventually eliminate the need for our government-run postal system! Your electronic house will take care of everything from calling up a plumber to fix its pipes to waking you up in the morning. We will even have electronic cows one day! The cows aren't too happy about it which is another reason why cows do not smile.

JUNGLE GENETICS

Early in this century, many fortunes such as Andrew Carnegie's were made in the steel industry. Genetic engineering holds the same promise during the rhinocerotic revolution. A relatively new science, biological industry, will create many opportunities during the coming years as new discoveries are made. Alvin Toffler in his book "The Third Wave" tells of scientists "studying the idea of utilizing

"Soon every home in the jungle will have a computer!"

bacteria capable of converting sunlight into electrochemical energy." Toffler also suggests that "biology will reduce or eliminate the need for oil in the production of plastics, fertilizers, clothes, paint, pesticides, and thousands of other products." He says that "genetic engineering will be employed to increase the world food supply."

Wow! Between the demand for new energies, the takeover of computers and the development of genetic engineering, the jungle is going to be a busy place. You are going to have to be a rhino to keep up with it all! Forget worrying about vultures and bugs eating you should you start to slow down . . . now you should be concerned about being replaced by a computer or being biologically altered!

POLITICIANS: AN ENDANGERED SPECIES

As the young, revolutionary rhinos of today and tomorrow begin to involve themselves in these exciting new industries, while revolting against the liberal views of the new older generation, the drive toward a laissez-faire free enterprise system will begin. Unlike yesterday's flower child, the new generation will strive towards individualism, independence, and a desire to take chances. The government of today does not foster these ideals and will, therefore, be rejected.

A bloated government, breeder of the supercow, will one day be a memory of the past. The career politician will be a forgotten, outdated, and disused relic as the bureaucracies crumble from their own weight. Life in the jungle will again throb with the impulse of achievement because the incentive will be there. The chance to improve one's own position in the jungle (The American Dream) will live again and the United Jungles of America will remain the greatest country in the world.

Chapter 10

JUNGLE EDUCATION

That last chapter was pretty heavy, huh? It's not like me to write such serious stuff, but I feel that it is imperative to the future of the rhino to end the power of the supercow. Rhinos are near extinction now! If we don't do something quick, animals of the future will only know the rhino by seeing us stuffed in a museum!

This book, I am sure, will be more controversial than "Rhinoceros Success" because I am presenting my views on some sensitive areas. I realize that some of my thoughts will be rejected by some of my fellow rhinos and applauded by others. I know what the cows will be thinking, which is all right, because everyone is entitled to his own opinion.

Though I am sure that there are some who would argue that point with me also.

NOBODY AGREES ON ANYTHING

Last year, I attended a mail order seminar that had the three top mail order millionaires present to reveal the supposed proper way to start and build a business in mail order. These guys were supposed to be the experts, right? I paid money to hear them!

Well, right from the start they began to disagree. One said using a P.O. box is fine, while the others disagreed. One condoned lots of copy and the others condemned it. They argued about products, mailing labels, advertisements and finally they argued about the admission price that we had been charged to come in and hear them!

I didn't learn much about mail order but I did learn a lot about animal behavior. And, believe me, these guys were animals by the time the seminar was over! I learned that no matter what your views are, there will ALWAYS be SOMEBODY who will disagree. The subject does not matter. Get the experts together on religion and they will disagree. Assemble the world's finest politicians and they will all argue. Gather the world's most experienced chicken breeders and they will debate chicken breeding techniques. Get the idea? It seems that no one can agree on anything except disagreement and there are those who will disagree with that! Whew!

STICK TO YOUR HORNS

I am no exception. I have strong views on certain subjects that I KNOW I AM RIGHT on! No one will ever convince me otherwise. "Stick to your guns" my grandmother always tells me. Well, everyone knows that rhinos do not carry guns, we carry horns. So "stick to your horns!" (It just doesn't have as nice of a ring to it though, does it?)

Nevertheless, stick to them anyway. You can't please everyone. To try to is only a lesson in frustration. Rhinos make up their own minds. Don't be like the mindless mass of cattle and sheep whose brains are like mush. Think for yourself. You are the expert on what YOU think and believe. Never let anyone try to control that for you. The first steps toward socialism and then communism are to control everyone's thoughts.

SHOOT THE MULE

Just because everyone else is being a cow doesn't mean that you have to be one too. That kind of "me too" thinking can really get you into trouble as Billy Martin tells in his autobiography entitled "Number 1." He remembers going down to Texas with Mickey Mantle to hunt on a friend's ranch. They arrived at the ranch house after a five hour drive and Mickey went in to check with the owner of the ranch while Billy waited outside in the car.

The owner granted them permission and asked Mickey if he would do him a favor. There was an old pet mule who was going blind and the owner didn't have the heart to kill the poor fellow, so he asked Mickey if he would do it for him. Mickey agreed to shoot the old mule.

On the way out of the house, heading back to the car where Billy was waiting, Mickey came up with an idea for a practical joke to play on Billy. He jumped in the car, slammed the door shut, put a scowl across his face and let Billy know that he was really mad. Billy asked, "What's the matter?"

Mickey replied, "He won't let us hunt here and I am so mad that I'm going to go by the barn and shoot his mule."

"Mickey, you can't shoot that man's mule," Billy protested. But Mickey insisted that nothing was going to stop him as they drove down to the barnyard. They found the mule and both Mickey and Billy jumped out of the car. Mickey raised his rifle and shot the old mule dead. Then he turned around and saw Billy with his rifle smoking. "What are you doing?" Mickey asked and Billy answered, "I got two of his cows."

ALTERNATIVE TO COLLEGE

Another example of "me too" thinking is the mass migration of kids right out of high school into college. My parents wanted me to have the same handicap every one else had, so they tried to send me to college too. Just kidding! I couldn't resist slipping that line in.

Seriously though, I would like to propose an alternative to rushing right into college, especially for kids who are not really sure what they want to do with their lives. Of course, if you want to be a doctor, dentist, lawyer, teacher or anything else that requires a college education, get your butt in gear and go. If you're not sure what you want to do but you have the opportunity to attend college and you *want* to go, then make sure you're signed up.

But if you plan on reluctantly attending college because your parents want you to go, or just because all your friends are going, don't waste the money. When I got out of high school, my parents wanted me to go to college and I asked them why. They said, "So you can get a better job." YIPES! I knew then that I did not want to go to college.

To me, there is no such thing as a "better job." I had already made up my mind to be the jungle entrepreneur. Sure, I might not be able to get myself a secure job, but I would be able to provide others with secure jobs.

Somebody has to hire the college kids, right? Kim and I both opted for adventure rather than security anyway.

BEGINNING CAPITALISM

I figured that I didn't need to go to college to learn how to become an entrepreneur. Besides, there were no "Beginning Capitalism" classes available. Just as the public schools do not encourage entrepreneurs, neither do most of the colleges and universities teach the advantages of our free enterprise system, although that is starting to change now as the rhinocerotic revolution gets underway. Again, there are some professional cows involved whose best interests would not be served by teaching capitalism.

William E. Simon, a supercow turned rhino (former Secretary of the Treasury), says that "America's major universities are today churning out young collectivists by legions." Simon, in his book "A Time for Truth" explains, "There was a time, 40 or 50 years ago, when capitalism *was* the dominant orthodoxy, not just in government and in the market place but in our universities as well. At that time, it was urged that it was for the good of the society as a whole that the dissonant voice be heard on those campuses—that the critic of capitalism, the dissenter from its philosophy, its economics, its mores be given a hearing—

and, characteristically, capitalism responded by doing precisely that. Indeed, it is through the very generosity and tolerance of capitalism that the enemies of capitalism have come to dominate our campuses today."

Perhaps a few years down the road, during the rhinocerotic revolution, when young rhinos will become fed up with socialist leanings and demand a move toward a laissez-faire capitalistic system, capitalism will again become the dominant orthodoxy. In fact, there are now at least four colleges around the country offering a major in entrepreneurial studies.

NO ALIMONY

Really though, the best time to experiment with being an entrepreneur is right after high school when you are young. You can go to college any time during your life, but to start a business you need that abundance of energy that you have when you're young. Recently, I met a 17 year old rhino named Scott Mahfouz who has been running his own business since he was 14 years old. He started a tape duplication and mail order business. Before he even graduated from high school he had his school friends working for him! He is saving for a Rolls-Royce now and I expect him to come tooling up our street in it sometime within the next few years.

What better time to start your own business than when you are young and have no family commitments? There are no babies to feed (hopefully) and no wife or husband to report to. A note of caution: make sure that when you do get married, you latch on to a grade AAA certified, charging rhinoceros because you don't want to be dragging some cow behind you. You will both be miserable. Intercultural marriages can be difficult. To avoid frustration, cows should marry cows and the rhinos should marry rhinos.

Usually, when you first get out of high school, you don't have too many financial obligations such as mortgage payments, kid's braces, and alimony. That allows you to put your time and energy into a business without starving to death in the beginning. Maybe the folks will let you stay at home until you get things rolling.

MEGABUCKS INCORPORATED

Keep in mind that I'm not talking about starting a giant, megabucks corporation. You have to start out small. It might even be a part time business while you are going to college. I started washing cars and helping Kim clip poodles. You can go to the library and get books that detail small business opportunities which you can start for less than $500, or you can come up with your own idea.

Another good way to get started is with your own Amway business. That can cost you practically nothing and within a few years you could be earning more per month than your friends spent on their entire college education. Seriously, I personally know rhinos who make astronomical sums of money in businesses such as these. Amway is a particularly good one too, because the company's founders, Jay Van Andel and Rich DeVos, are firm supporters of our free enterprise system and the Amway business reflects that.

TEST YOUR HORNS

When you're young, you are flexible, you are not financially committed, you have more energy and, generally, you are more audacious because you really don't have anything to lose. When our dog grooming business failed, my kids didn't starve because I didn't have any kids. My credit was not blemished because I had no credit to start with. I wasn't the social outcast of the community because I was just a kid!

Maybe you could try a year of college and then a year of testing your horns out in the jungle. Do whatever feels best for you, just make sure that you DO something! And for you rhinos who have been out of high school or college for a number of years, don't let that discourage you from taking an entrepreneurial

"Make sure that when you do get married, you latch on to a grade AAA certified, charging rhinoceros."

safari. You have thicker skin and you are not
ready for the pasture yet!

Chapter 11

EPILOGUE

It is amazing how much you can learn by reading the dictionary, isn't it? Here's an interesting word I came across the other day—epilimnion. It turns out that in any heated body of water there are three layers. The upper, lighter and warmer layer which is oxygen-rich is called the epilimnion. The next layer is the thermocline. This is a thin layer that separates the epilimnion from the lower, colder, heavier, and oxygen-poor layer. Now I am going crazy because I cannot find out what that colder, bottom layer is called! If you know, I would greatly appreciate your sending me a postcard to fill me in.

Anyway, not to get too far off the track, right after the word "epilimnion," I came across the word "Epilogue—a concluding section that rounds out the design of a literary work." Immediately I thought, "That is what I have *got* to have in my book!" Now here it is. You are reading it! To think that just last month it was only a word in a dictionary. It kind of gives you tingly feelings all over, doesn't it?

SHIVERING TINGLES

It gives me tingly feelings but I am not sure that they are from bringing an epilogue to life. I think my tingles are actually trembles from thinking about how some animals out in the jungle are going to react to this book . . . like my Dad who works for the government. How is he going to feel about being labeled a supercow? What about Kim's parents who both went through college and believe that a college education is highly desirable? They probably won't talk to me after reading my "college may be hazardous to your health" theory.

Maybe the tingles turned trembles are from imagining the government's response to "Advanced Rhinocerology." I am liable to have the IRS, the CIA, and the FBI trying to lock me up in prison for attempting to overthrow the government. How is the pastor of our church going to feel about God being illustrated as a rhinoceros? I could be excommunicated! My trembling tingles could be from the thought of having the union leaders after me for creating labor unrest. What if EVERYBODY quits their job and NOBODY shows up for work tomorrow? I could be in trouble!

HOW DID THIS HAPPEN?

Really, I just started out with the idea that I would write another simple motivational book to follow "Rhinoceros Success." I don't know what happened. It started out innocently enough with the premise that it is a jungle out there and somehow, I ended up alienating my whole market. Now who is going to buy my book? I have certainly eliminated a lot of potential buyers with my ramblings about the need for trimming down the bureaucracy. "Advanced Rhinocerology" will definitely not be on the list of books to read for all the civil service workers. What kind of company is going to distribute my book to all their employees and risk having them quit to start their own companies? What church pastor is going to recommend my book when I refer to God as "your safari guide?"

"Advanced Rhinocerology" will no doubt be banned from all the colleges and universities, and the postal employees are liable to refuse to deliver anything with my name on it. Egads! How did all this happen? Even my dear old Dad, whom I love so much, will probably throw his complimentary copy in the trash and then dump coffee grounds on top of it.

Oh well, no one said it was going to be easy!

**REMEMBER THAT LIFE IS
AN ADVENTURE.
GO LIVE IT!**

Photos by Mike Thompson

ABOUT THE AUTHOR

Scott Alexander is a rhinoceros (species—ceratotherium simum). Often sighted in Laguna Hills, California, he is mostly active in the morning and evening. Although a solitary animal, Scott is occasionally seen wallowing in the mud with his beautiful wife, Kimber (also species ceratotherium simum).

Weighing in at 6,135 pounds, Scott trots at a speed of 18 m.p.h., but can hit over 25 m.p.h. when pressed. He feeds entirely on grass, and reliable accounts last indicate that Scott's horn measured over five feet long. He is approximately 25 years old.

HAVE YOU READ "RHINOCEROS SUCCESS"?

Scott Alexander's first book, "Rhinoceros Success" is the book that started the whole rhinoceros mania. It is required reading for all rhinoceroses, and it wouldn't hurt a few cows to read it either.

If you cannot find it in your favorite bookstore, let them know that they are blowing it. Then send a check or money order to The Rhino's Press for $5.95. (That already includes tax and postage.) We would love to send you a copy! And of course, if you would like additional copies of "Advanced Rhinocerology," you may also order them directly from us for $5.95 each. (Tax and postage already included.)

We also offer quantity discounts of both "Rhinoceros Success" and "Advanced Rhinocerology" with bulk purchase for educational, business or sales promotion use.

Send your order or request for more information to:

The Rhino's Press, Inc.
P.O. Box 3520
Laguna Hills, CA 92654
Ph. (714) 997-3217
Outside California call 1-800-8-SAFARI

Hi Rhinos!

☐ Please send me your free Rhinoceros Newsletter.

☐ Please send me information on quantity discounts for your books.

☐ Please send me your free rhino catalog.

Name _____

Address _____

City _____ State _____ Zip _____

Ph. _____